CRAFT TOPICS

PIRATES

FACTS ● THINGS TO MAKE ● ACTIVITIES

RACHEL WRIGHT

SEA-TO-SEA

Mankato Collingwood London

This edition first published in 2005 by
Sea-to-Sea Publications
1980 Lookout Drive
North Mankato
Minnesota 56003

Copyright © Sea-to-Sea Publications 2005

ISBN   1-932889-06-X

Printed in China

Library of Congress Control Number: 2004103598

2 4 6 8 9 7 5 3

Published by arrangement with the Watts Publishing Group Ltd, London

CONTENTS

THE STORY OF PIRATES

Pirates are sea robbers. Throughout history they have terrorized the world's seas. Wherever there have been ships with goods worth stealing, there have been pirates.

THE GOLDEN AGE OF PIRACY

The 1600's and early 1700's were known as the Golden Age of Piracy. Two earlier events had greatly changed the history of piracy. One was the discovery of a sea route from Europe to India. The other was the discovery of America.

These finds opened up an exciting new world for European trade. Ships were sent to India, Arabia and America. There they were loaded with goods such as gold, tobacco, silks and spices, and then sailed back to Europe. Not surprisingly, the temptation to rob these ships of their new found wealth was one that many could not resist.

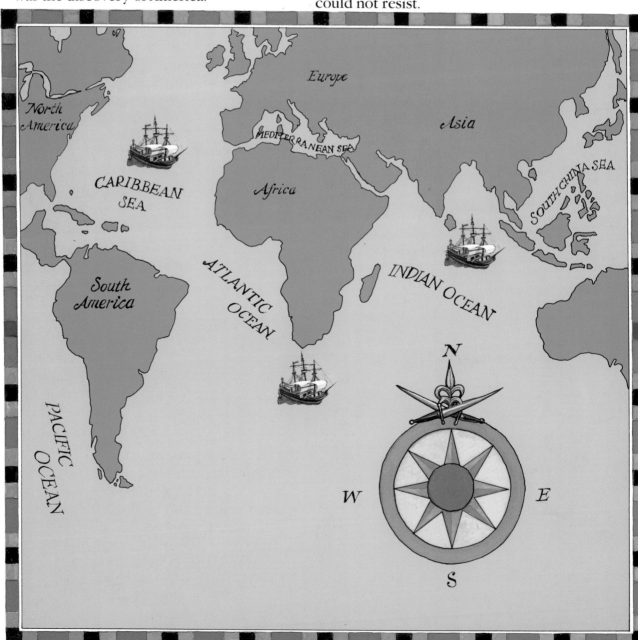

WHY DID PIRATES BECOME PIRATES?

Pirate life was hard, but life ashore could be worse. Many men ran away to sea to escape the misery of poverty and unemployment back home.

A number of sailors, sick of the harsh discipline of navy life, were lured by the freedom and adventure piracy offered. Others were recruited from merchant ships captured by pirates.

On the whole, most would-be pirates were tempted by the prospect of earning lots of cash quickly.

PIRATE TREASURE

On the whole, pirates tended not to attack ships carrying gold and precious jewels. Treasure ships were usually accompanied by a well armed escort, which made attacks upon them difficult.

Instead, pirates favored merchant ships, carrying silks, spices, tobacco or timber which the pirates could then sell at a nearby port. They could also use the captured ship as their own.

If a ship under attack were carrying an important passenger, he or she could be taken for ransom too.

THE END OF THE GOLDEN AGE

Throughout the Golden Age, some of the most ruthless pirates of all wreaked havoc on the high seas. If ever there was a time to be a pirate, this was it.

By about 1740, however, things had changed. European countries had begun to co-operate with each other in their battle against piracy. They started to police the seas more efficiently and passed tougher piracy laws. No longer welcome at their favorite ports, pirates gradually found it harder and harder to continue their trade.

Piracy did not die out with the passing of this Golden Age. Far from it! In fact, there are still a small number of pirates at work today, particularly in the seas around Borneo and Indonesia. However, because some of the most famous and thrilling pirates of all lived during the Golden Age, much that you'll read in this book dates back to that time.

Piracy through the ages

In 78 BC Mediterranean pirates held Julius Caesar to ransom. After his release, Caesar returned to recover his money. Centuries later, piracy could still be found in the Mediterranean.

Between the years 834 and 930, Vikings regularly attacked coastal towns in England and Ireland. They sailed in huge ships with long oars. Each oar needed up to four men to pull it.

Full of tiny islands with hidden bays, the Caribbean Sea made the perfect pirate hideaway. During the Golden Age, trading ships sailing from South America often fell foul of pirates here.

Today, bands of pirates trawl busy waterways such as the South China Sea. Over half the world's supertankers pass through the sea, and piracy is on the rise.

FAMOUS PIRATES

BLACKBEARD

One of the most dreaded pirates of all was Edward Teach, or Blackbeard. To make himself look terrifying during a raid, he used to braid lit hemp fuses (used to light cannons) into his hair and beard. These fuses burned slowly and smoked. His frightened enemies must have thought his head was on fire!

Between 1716 and 1718, Blackbeard attacked trading ships off the North American coast. He smuggled their goods ashore and sold them off cheaply.

The governor of Virginia eventually sent two navy ships to capture him and after a long battle, Blackbeard was killed.

CAPTAIN BARTHOLOMEW ROBERTS

Bartholomew Roberts was probably the most successful pirate of all time. Between 1719 and 1722, he captured more than 400 ships off the coasts of West Africa and Canada and in the Caribbean Sea.

Although cruel to prisoners, he was a deeply religious man. And strict, too! He banned his crew from gambling and insisted lights were out below deck by 8 o'clock. He hated alcohol. His favorite drink was a cup of tea! Stranger still, he liked to wear fine clothes, even in battle!

Roberts died fighting and, as he had ordered, his crew threw his dead body overboard, fine clothes and all.

ANNE BONNY

Pirate rules did not allow any woman on board ship. But this did not stop Anne Bonny! She was an Irish girl who fell in love with a pirate captain called Calico Jack Rackham. He agreed that she could join him at sea, but only on condition that she dressed and worked like a man, and told no one her secret.

In 1719, Rackham captured a Dutch merchant ship and took on board a young English sailor. Anne fell in love with this sailor only to discover that he was in fact a she, by the name of Mary Read. The two women soon became firm friends and proved to be fearsome fighters.

MARY READ

For some reason, Mary Read had been brought up as a boy. Before joining Rackham's crew she had worked as a boy servant, a soldier and a sailor.

In 1720, Rackham's ship was attacked and captured, just off Jamaica. Mary and Anne were among the last pirates left fighting on deck. All their fellow crew mates had died or were hiding below.

Once on shore, Rackham's crew were sentenced to death. Both women, however, were pregnant and so were spared. They returned to their cells where Mary caught a fever and died.

BARBAROSSA

During the first part of the 1500's, two Turkish brothers ruled piracy in the Mediterranean Sea. They both had red beards and so were named Barbarossa, which means "red beard."

They led men from parts of North Africa and from Turkey in attacks upon European ships. Because they attacked Christian ships and towns, they won the support of fellow Muslims.

Arouj Barbarossa died in battle, but Khair-ed-Din lived to become a rich and famous Turkish hero.

DRESS LIKE A PIRATE

Pirates tended to wear the same type of clothes on ship that they would have worn ashore. Here are some ideas of ways to dress like a pirate. See if you can add any other ideas of your own too.

You'll need to wear something loose so that you won't have any trouble climbing the rigging. How about starting with a pair of plain, comfortable pants or jeans, and a baggy shirt, belted at the waist? You could tie a piece of cloth around your head or make a hat like this.

2. Cut it out and add a piratical symbol. Be careful not to cut along the fold. Finish by gluing the two ends together.

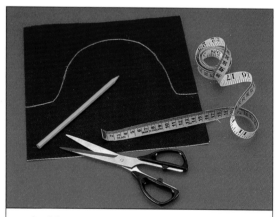

1. Measure around your head and cut a piece of cardboard the same length. Fold the cardboard in half and draw the shape of your hat.

3. If you injured an eye in battle, you would need an eye patch. Cut a shape like this from a piece of thin black cardboard and thread a loop of elastic through.

Pirates believed that earrings helped their eyesight. They used the gold to pay for funerals, too!

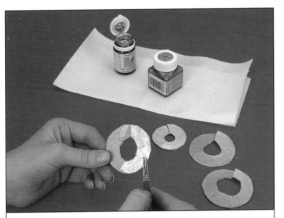

4. Cut a hoop of thick cardboard like this. Add a notch long enough to slip over your ear. Now, paint your earring silver or gold.

You'll also need some weapons. Draw daggers and cutlasses onto thick cardboard and cut them out. Cover with silver foil and colored cardboard, or if you prefer, use paint.

PIRATICAL DUTIES

Life aboard a pirate ship was not totally wild. Crews often drew up a set of rules called articles, which every member had to obey. Here are some of the articles agreed to by Bartholomew Roberts' crew:

Articles

1. All important decisions to be put to a vote.
2. Any man caught stealing shall be marooned. (This usually meant being left on a deserted shore with only a gun, some shot, a bottle of gunpowder and some water.)
3. All pistols and cutlasses to be kept clean.
4. No women allowed on board.
5. Any man who deserts ship in battle shall be put to death or marooned.
6. No striking one another on board ship. All quarrels to be settled on shore.
7. The captain and quartermaster to receive two shares of a prize; the master gunner, and boatswain, one and a half shares; other officers one and a quarter shares; all others, one share each. (Pirates earned only what they stole.)
8. Injuries to be compensated. Any man who loses a limb in service shall receive £400.

Although their ships belonged to the entire crew, and most decisions were put to a vote, pirates still appointed officers.

The captain was usually chosen by his men, who were free to sack him at any time. His commands went unchallenged during raids only. Apart from an extra share of booty, he had few privileges.

The quartermaster was next in command. Elected by the crew, he shared out the booty and punished troublemakers.

The lieutenant took charge if the captain was killed.

The boatswain looked after the day to day running of the ship, while the sailingmaster was responsible for the navigation and setting of the sails.

A ship's surgeon and carpenter had very similar tools. This meant that if there was no surgeon on board, the carpenter had to perform amputations instead. Rather unfortunate for the poor patients, particularly since they had no anesthetics to put them to sleep.

The master gunner kept an eye on the gun crew. Theirs was the noisiest and most dangerous job of all. The huge cannons they used were secured to the ship's side with strong ropes called breeching ropes. When fired, these cannons would rebound violently, putting tremendous strain on their breeching ropes. With continuous firing this rebounding got worse. At each shot, the back part of the cannon would leap up to the beams above. The breeching ropes might then snap, leaving 2-3 tons of cannon free to roll about the deck. Little wonder gun crews often made wills to each other as they went into battle!

Once on board an enemy ship, pirates fought with hand weapons. They used...

daggers for stabbing

cutlasses for slicing

pikes for thrusting

pistols for shooting.

Pirate Ships

In general, pirates sailed in merchant ships. These were smaller and swifter than the heavy galleons many pirates tried to plunder.

Once they'd captured a merchant ship, pirates often altered it to suit their needs. They built up the gunwales to protect themselves during battle. They also removed the bulkheads, the walls dividing up the inside of a ship, to give themselves more room.

Pirates rarely remained loyal to one ship only. In fact, they changed ship as often as need demanded or opportunity allowed.

Here is a cutaway of Captain William Kidd's ship, *Adventure Galley*. Although not a merchant ship, she was fast, fairly easy to maneuver and a good fighting vessel.

Launched in 1696, *Adventure Galley* was designed to attack and capture pirate ships. Her captain, however, had other ideas. Instead of chasing pirates, Kidd decided to become a pirate himself. He sailed to the Indian Ocean, joined up with some other pirates and began plotting and plundering. Before long, *Adventure Galley* had become a pirate ship — and a very successful one too.

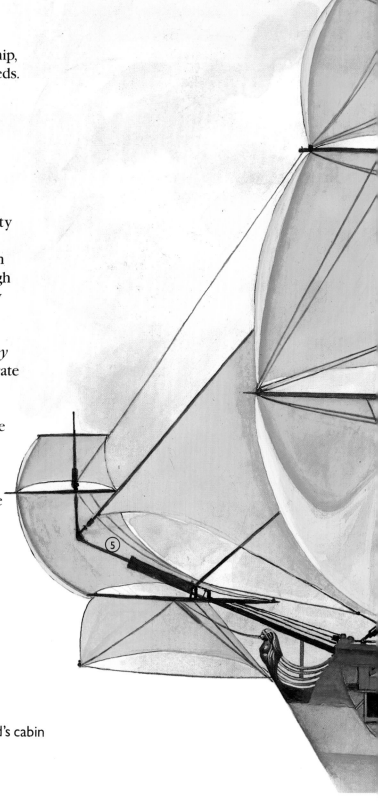

1. Main mast
2. Fore mast
3. Mizzen mast
4. Crow's nest
5. Bowsprit
6. Galley
7. Shot
8. Hold
9. Capstan
10. Gunwale
11. Bilge
12. Gun deck
13. Captain Kidd's cabin

FIGUREHEADS

Many of the ships captured by pirates had figureheads. These were carved figures usually found below the bowsprit, at the front of a ship. A lot of sailors thought that these figureheads had special powers.

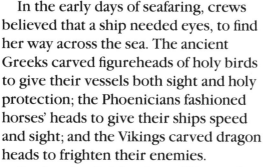

In the early days of seafaring, crews believed that a ship needed eyes, to find her way across the sea. The ancient Greeks carved figureheads of holy birds to give their vessels both sight and holy protection; the Phoenicians fashioned horses' heads to give their ships speed and sight; and the Vikings carved dragon heads to frighten their enemies.

During the Golden Age of Piracy, the lion was a popular figurehead on warships. Perhaps this was because sailors hoped that their ship would inherit the strength and majesty of a lion.

Figureheads representing the name of a ship eventually replaced the lion. During the 1800's, the figure of a bare breasted woman became more popular still. Although women were considered unlucky aboard ship, a naked woman was thought to have been able to calm storms at sea.

When steamships replaced sailing ships, figureheads became less common. Few ships have figureheads today.

MAKE YOUR OWN SHIP'S FIGUREHEAD

You will need: modeling clay
● newspaper ● petroleum jelly
● glue ● glue brush ● paintbrush
● poster paints ● colored paper.

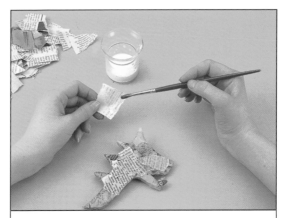

2. Brush a coat of glue over the newspaper and add another layer of paper. Keep doing this until your figurehead is the size you want it.

3. Let it dry thoroughly. Then paint it with thick poster paints or decorate with tiny pieces of colored paper.

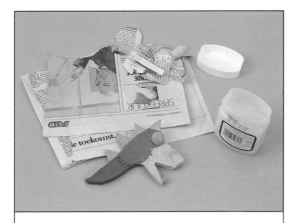

1. Model a figurehead in clay. Spread petroleum jelly over your model and then cover it evenly with small pieces of newspaper.

THE JOLLY ROGER

Pirates in the West Indies were the first to fly red flags to let everyone know who they were. Other pirates flew whichever country's flag seemed most sensible at the time! It wasn't until about 1700 that the famous skull and crossbones first appeared on a pirate flag. The skull and crossbones was a popular symbol of death which often appeared on gravestones at that time. Imagine how merchant seamen must have felt when they saw this gruesome image fluttering towards them!

Bartholomew Roberts' flag.

Pirate captains created their own pirate flag, or Jolly Roger as it was called. Blackbeard added an hourglass to show that time was running out for his victims. Others added cutlasses, daggers and bleeding hearts.

Sometimes they would fly a Jolly Roger to give their chosen victim the chance to surrender. If this offer was refused, the pirates flew a red flag instead which meant . . . PREPARE TO DIE!!

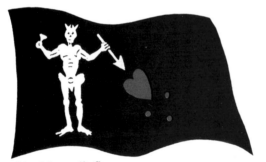

Blackbeard's flag.

The Jolly Roger was also known as Black Jack or the Banner of King Death.

Henry Every's flag.

To make a Jolly Roger, trace the symbol below onto some cardboard and cut out the shape. Draw around your cardboard cut-out onto a piece of white felt. Cut this cloth shape out and glue it onto a square of black felt. To complete your flag, tape a stick down one side.

Did you know a Yellow Jack was flown when a ship had disease on board?

Calico Jack Rackham's flag.

PIRATE LIFE

For any pirate who misbehaved, there was BIG trouble in store.

Flogging was the most common punishment for all sailors. The unfortunate offender would be whipped, or flogged, with the cat o' nine tails. This was a wooden stick with nine knotted tails of rope attached.

Another typical punishment was to stuff a man's mouth with oakum, strands of rope soaked in tar, and then set it alight.

Keelhauling was equally nasty. This involved tying a length of rope around a man, dropping him overboard, and then dragging him under the ship, to the other side. This really hurt because as he was pulled, his back or chest would scrape against the barnacles on the ship's hull. Terrible punishments such as these awaited all sailors, not just pirates.

18

To unwind after a hard day spent torturing each other, pirates liked to sing, dance, play cards and dice (a good excuse for a bit of gambling), and get drunk. They also repaired and cleaned the ship and mended their clothes — not as much fun, but better than being tortured!

One thing pirates at sea rarely did was linger over a scrumptious supper. Food eaten on long sea voyages was always revolting. Supplies of fresh food ran out quickly. Meat and fish had to be heavily salted so that they would keep. Instead of bread, which went stale too quickly, pirates ate plain biscuits. These soon became infested with weevils, and had to be eaten in the dark so that the poor pirates weren't put off by watching their dinner writhing about. Sometimes these biscuits became so hard it was easier to carve ornaments out of them than eat them. Rum and brandy were the main pirate drinks because, unlike beer and water, they kept well.

It's no wonder that pirates were often ill. Their wooden sailing ships were damp, dark, and stank of bilge water. They were overcrowded and often overrun with rats and bugs, too. These conditions, together with a lack of fresh food and water, led to terrible illness. On a long voyage, pirate captains expected to lose nearly half their crew to diseases such as typhus, malaria, yellow fever and scurvy. This is why pirates were often more interested in capturing another ship's medicine chest than anything else.

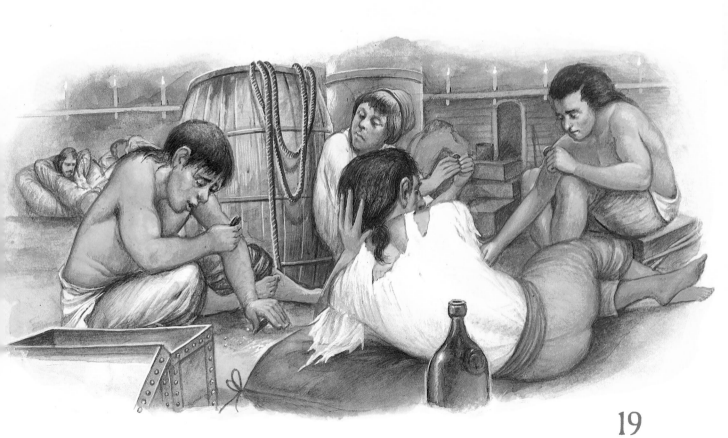

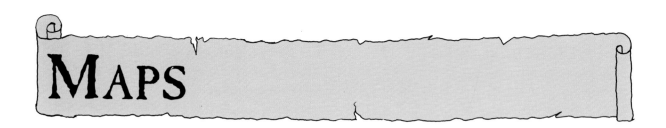

MAPS

Most pirates spent what they made as fast as they could. Only a few had treasure enough worth burying.

Those that did usually made a detailed map to remind themselves where they had left their loot. After all, if a pirate couldn't remember the exact spot upon his return, his fortune would be lost forever!

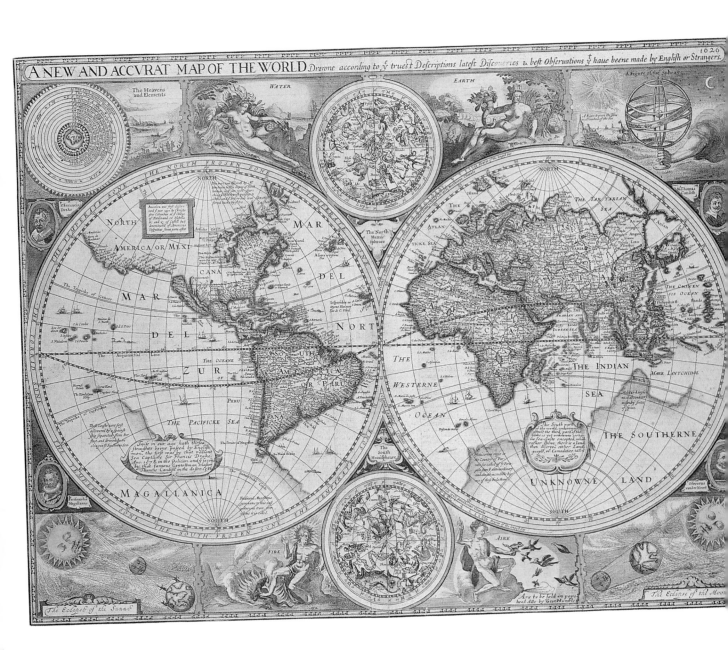

MAPMAKING

You will need: paper
● waterproof pens or colored pencils
● a used tea bag ● cooking oil and
paintbrush ● paper towels.

2. To make your map look ancient, tear the edges slightly. Gently wipe both sides with a used, damp tea bag. Crumple the map into a ball and leave it to dry.

3. When your map is dry, uncurl it, put it on a sheet of paper, and brush it carefully with cooking oil. Then blot it dry with paper towels. It should now look and feel more like genuine parchment.

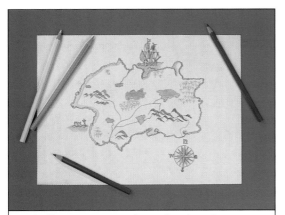

1. Draw a map of an island and choose where you would bury your treasure. Don't forget landmarks such as trees, mountains and rivers. They will help to guide you.

Did you know that Blackbeard is said to have buried treasure on a remote island and then left one of his fourteen wives there, alone, to guard it?

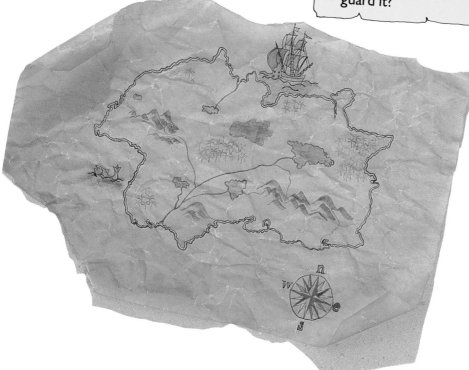

BAKE A PIRATE ISLAND

You will need: poster paints and brushes ● plastic drinking straws ● old pasta shells or dried beans ● toothpicks ● colored cardboard ● tissue paper ● glue.
Island dough recipe: 1 cup all-purpose flour; 6 tablespoons salt; 2 tablespoons of cooking oil; water; mixing bowl. You will also need to ask an adult to help you.

1. Mix the flour and salt in a large mixing bowl. Add the oil and just enough water to make a soft dough. Knead well and then divide the dough into two lumps.

2. Shape one lump into an island. You might like to add mountains, rock pools and caves — or even a hidden bay where your ship could lurk, ready for a surprise attack. Use the remaining dough to make a skeleton, a ship or anything else you might find on or near a pirate island.

3. Ask an adult to line a cookie sheet with foil and bake your models in the oven for about 25 minutes at 350°F. If you want them rock hard, leave them in a little longer.

4. When your models have cooled, start painting. Decorate your beaches with dried beans or painted pasta shells. Draw bones onto your skeleton!

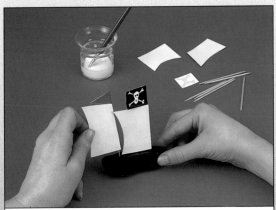

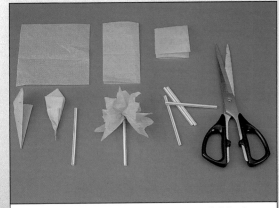

5. If you made a ship base, cut out sail-shaped pieces of cardboard and glue them onto toothpicks. Now, stick them into your ship. Don't forget to add a pirate flag!

6. To make palm trees, twist folded squares of tissue paper into shortened straws. Open out the paper slightly and tear the edges to make it look more like leaves. If your island is very hard, gently drill a hole in it with a toothpick. Then plant your palm tree in the hole.

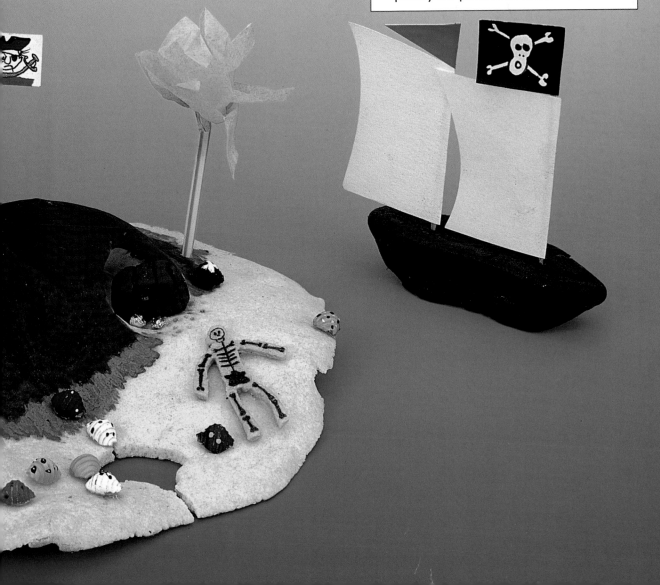

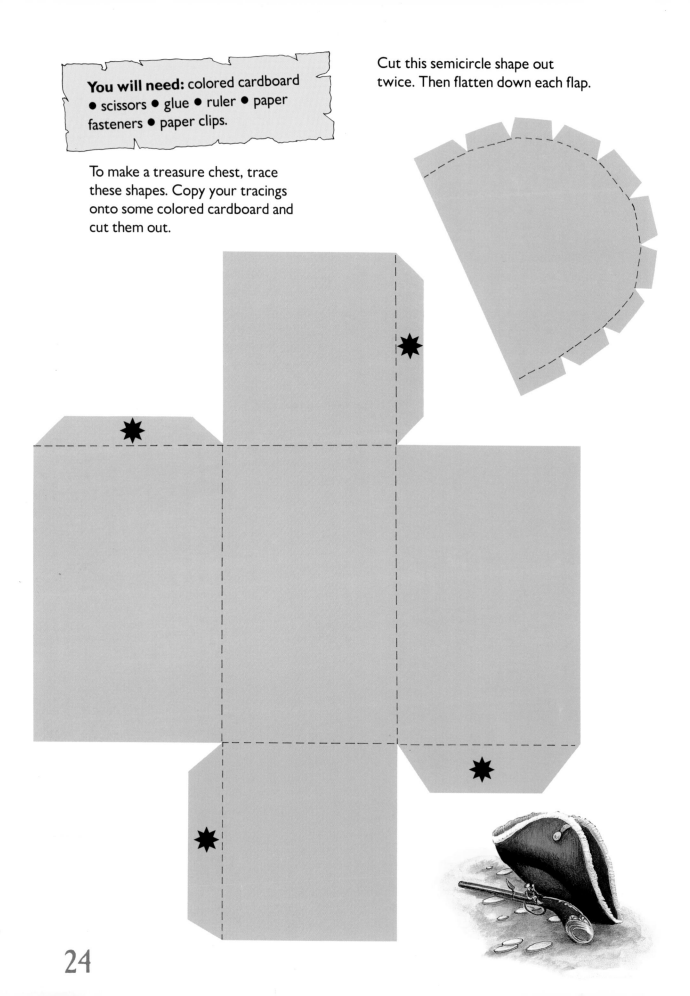

You will need: colored cardboard
● scissors ● glue ● ruler ● paper
fasteners ● paper clips.

To make a treasure chest, trace
these shapes. Copy your tracings
onto some colored cardboard and
cut them out.

Cut this semicircle shape out
twice. Then flatten down each flap.

TREASURE CHEST

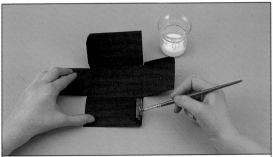

1. To make a box, glue the back of each flap marked * onto its nearest panel.

2. To make the lid, cut a rectangle of cardboard 5½ in by 3¼ in. Put a strip of glue along one of the longer sides.

3. Holding your rectangle like this, stick it to the flaps of one of your semicircles.

4. It helps if you paper clip these two pieces together while waiting for the glue to dry. Now, glue the other semicircle into place.

5. When your lid is dry, use paper fasteners to attach it to the chest.

6. Decorate the chest with strips of a different colored cardboard affixed with paper fasteners.

KNOTS

If you worked on a sailing ship you really did have to "know the ropes." The masts and sails were controlled by a mass of ropes called rigging. Like all sailors, pirates needed to know exactly where each rope was and how it was tied. Here are two knots the pirates in this book might have used.

The Reef Knot — good for joining two ends of rope over a reefed, or rolled up, sail.

The Cat's Paw — ideal for attaching a rope to a hook.

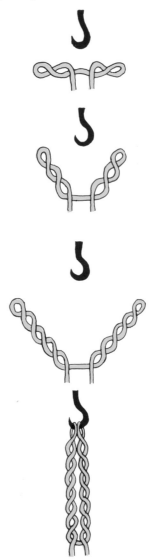

To measure the speed of their sailing ships, pirates of old would probably have used a log line. This was a length of cord, knotted at equal spaces, with a wooden board attached to one end. The board was thrown into the sea. It held the end of the cord steady while the ship sailed on. As the cord unraveled, the pirate holding it would have to count how many knots passed through his fingers in a given time. Each knot equaled the speed of one nautical mile an hour.

CHANTIES

Chanties were work songs, sung by sailors. The earliest ones we know about are well over 200 years old.

With their strong simple rhythms, chanties helped sailors keep in time with each other as they worked.

Different chanties accompanied different tasks. Some with long repetitive rhythms were sung when turning the capstan to haul up the anchor. Others with a short, jerky beat were better suited to working the pumps to get rid of water below deck.

One More Day

Paddy Doyle's Boots

DIFFERENT PIRATES

TRUE PIRATES

True pirates stole from anyone. They were criminals and if caught, faced certain death. Many British pirates ended up hanging from Execution Dock in Wapping, London. Their dead bodies were then chained up along the River Thames as a warning to anyone else thinking of doing a bit of pirating in their spare time.

BUCCANEERS

During the 1600's, a group of runaway men — slaves, criminals and refugees — were living in the Caribbean. Mainly English, French and Dutch, they were a wild, unruly bunch. They hated the Spanish, who ruled much of the Caribbean at that time, and so enjoyed plundering Spanish ships whenever they could.

Their name — buccaneers — came from the French word "boucaner," the name of the smoking process when cooking meat, that left a distinctive aroma on the men.

PRIVATEERS

Sailing in ships sponsored by their government back home, privateers had permission to rob ships from enemy countries. The only drawback was that if they managed to return to their own country, they had to share their stolen cargo with their sponsor.

Privateers carried documents called letters of marque. These letters could save them from punishment if their piratical attacks failed. It wasn't very fair because their crimes were like that of any other pirate.

DID YOU KNOW?

One of the few things pirate ships had in abundance was rope. So, apart from all its usual uses, pirates wiped their hands with it, greased it to use as candles and tarred strands of it and squeezed them between the ship's planks to stop leaking.

"Walking the plank" is the most famous piratical punishment that never was! There is no proof that this dastardly practice ever existed. Instead, it was probably dreamed up by Victorian storytellers. Or maybe the myth dates back to ancient Roman times when captives not worth holding to ransom were invited to swim back to shore.

Pirate ships didn't have a ship's cat, either. A cat would have eaten the ship's rats which the pirates might have wanted to eat themselves. After all, there's a lot of protein in a rat!

At the bottom of the Pacific Ocean, off the coast of South America, lies the largest pirate treasure of all. Hundreds of bits of silver, on board a Spanish ship, were captured by pirates. Mistaking them for tin, the pirate crew threw them overboard. It was later revealed that this lost booty was worth over $300,000!

At one time, Port Royal in Jamaica was a popular pirate haunt. But on June 7, 1692, a terrible disaster took place. An earthquake shook the town, the ground opened and whole streets disappeared. As if that was not enough, a huge tidal wave then rushed in and the whole town vanished. Even today divers still find relics from this lost town.

Did you know that all these are other names for a pirate?

Filibusterer
Freebooter
Corsair
Sea Rover

GLOSSARY

Amputate, to — to cut off, usually referring to an arm or leg. Sailors of old who had to have limbs amputated were often given swigs of alcohol to help numb the pain.

Articles — rules that pirates and privateers had to obey while on board ship. These rules included how any booty was to be divided, and how the ship's captain should be elected.

Barnacles — tiny hard-shelled creatures that cling to a ship's hull. To get rid of them, pirates had to beach their ships (preferably somewhere well hidden), turn them onto one side and scrape the barnacles off. This was called careening.

Bilge — the bottom of a ship. The bilge was packed with stone, which helped to keep the ship steady and upright.

Black Jack — another name for the pirate flag. A jack is a flag, especially one flown from the bowsprit of a ship.

Booty — stolen goods.

Bowsprit — a pole projecting from the bow, front part, of a ship.

Buccaneer — a pirate who preyed on Spanish shipping in the Caribbean during the 1600's and 1700's.

Capstan — a revolving wooden cylinder, used for winding up an anchor. Pushing the capstan around was tiring work.

Cargo — goods carried by a ship.

Cat o' nine tails — a whip with nine knotted ropes attached, used for punishing sailors. Those troublemakers who really misbehaved could be sentenced to one hundred lashes or more.

Galley — a ship which had both oars and sails; a ship's kitchen.

Gunwale (gunnel) — upper edge of a ship's side.

Hold — place where a ship's cargo is stored. Water barrels, salted meat, spare ropes and sails would all have been stored here.

Jolly Roger — a pirate flag. Some think that the name, Jolly Roger, may have come from *Old Roger*, another name for the devil. Others believe that it may have come from the French, *joli rouge,* meaning *pretty red* — a reference to the red flags buccaneers used to fly.

Letter of marque — a license, issued by a government, giving the bearer permission to rob enemy ships. These letters sometimes proved to be fakes. If caught with a fake letter, a privateer could be punished as a pirate.

Loot — stolen goods; plunder.

Maroon, to — to abandon someone on a desolate shore. Many pirates feared this punishment more than any other.

Oakum — strands of tarred rope that were squeezed between a ship's wooden planks to stop leaking. Unpicking ropes to make oakum was a very boring job.

Pike — a pointed pole, good for poking at an enemy as you boarded their ship.

Privateer — a person, or privately owned vessel, authorized to attack enemy ships. Two English privateers, Sir Francis Drake and Sir John Hawkins, were so successful that they were knighted by Queen Elizabeth I.

Prize — a captured ship; booty.

Rigging — system of ropes supporting a ship's masts and sails.

Yellow Jack — flag pirates flew when they had disease on board ship.

Weevil — a type of beetle.

RESOURCES

Places to visit

Though several pirates sailed off the New England, Long Island, and Florida coasts, for example, there are very few pirate artifacts found in the United States. You may want to try checking with local museums to see if they may be able to direct you to any pirate or pirate-related exhibits.

Peabody New England Maritime Museum of Salem
161 Essex Street
East India Square
Salem, Massachusetts 01970
(508) 745-1896
(Relics related to the pirates include pistols, cutlasses and cannon used in battle against pirates off the New England coast.

Museum of Florida History
500 S. Bruno
Tallahassee, Florida 32399-0250
(904) 488-1484
(The Shipwreck exhibit here has artifacts from Spanish treasure fleets, including the 1715 plate fleet and the 1733 plate fleet.

BOOKS TO READ

The Best Book of Pirates by Barnaby Howard (Boston; Kingfisher Books, 2002)

The History of Pirates by Angus Konstam (Guildford, CT; The Lyons Press, 2002)

Piracy and Plunder: A Murderous Business by Milton Meltor (New York; Dutton, 2001)

The Great Pirate Activity Book by Deri Roberts (Boston; Kingfisher, 1995)

Eyewitness: Pirate by Richard Platt (New York; DK Publishing, 2000)

The Amazing World of Pirates by Philip Steele (London; Lorenz Books, 2003)

ON THE WEB
www.piratesinfo.com
  (General information)
www.legends.dm.net/pirates
  (Pirate yarns and yore)
www.nationalgeographic.com/pirates
  (A treasure chest of information)

Index